Inward & Beyond

Transformation is a Conscious Choice

By Brenda R Bryan

ISBN 978-0-578-35568-9

Library of Congress Cataloguing-in-publishing

Why I created this book:

A few years ago, I read "Big Magic" by Elizabeth Gilbert. I was challenged by the chapter regarding people not listening when the magic of an idea is dropped into our minds, and we fail to act on it. I have always considered myself a creative, but at that time, I would not have called myself a writer. However, lines of poetry would pop into my head. I started to type them into my phone, sometimes it was just the one line, sometimes it was the whole poem.

I was going through a tough break up with a woman who fractured my heart wide open. And at the time, these words were finding a place of expression. I faced deep issues I had been aware of but not able to grasp for years. I explored what it was to say yes, with no expectations of the outcome.

The journey was a beautifully tortuous one. One that I am grateful for. I began the trek expressing the inner world that was unfolding. The pain, the darkness, the sorrow came pouring out.

I believe people possess a deep magic, and we never know how that magic will change us. I said yes; I knew the journey would be splendidly challenging. I knew the lessons unfolding required me to dig deep, take responsibility for my unconscious behavior, and learn radical self-care.

This process early on was to do healing work on myself. What started to come together was a very raw, vulnerable voice I had never articulated before. I found what became a voice looking for expression. When I started this process, it was not to publish a book. Called to share some of the work, I was drawn to the idea that this material would be healing.

I have been a transformational seeker for most of my life, but I am a very private woman, what is exposed here is a new stepping up to a voice of ownership. I believe the best teachers are role models. I teach the importance and strength of vulnerability. I teach that words matter. So, it matters very much to me that I walk my talk. That I show courage in sharing my shadow; that I show courage in sharing my light. I move forward with the intention of showing up differently than I ever have.

The poems and essays are tender to me. They are messages from Spirit to support my healing and growth. My greater work is to be part of healing our relationships. And by so doing we heal our society and the greater desire to heal our planet.

What I want now is for this book to reach hearts, to have a voice that encourages others to listen to that magic in their life and to have the guts to act on it. To listen and follow what Spirit wants to express through you. Everyone has this magic within them, everyone has a creative force wanting to be expressed. Only you can follow that nudge, only you can know what passion is waiting to find its expression.

My wish for you is that you off your ass and take action to live your life your way.

My passion is that this book will give me the courage to get out there and Raise My Voice to live a deeper truth of self- expression going forward.

Enjoy,

Brenda R Bryan

Dedication

To Sara who broke me into a thousand pieces so I could be liberated in ways that totally surprised me.

May all you who read this book say YES to the joy of transformation as a conscious choice.

I wish to thank Jennafer Morgan, Liz Earhart, and Pamala J. Vincent.

Contents

The Spark

Our time together was mostly filled with unmet promises.

What is it to follow a line of inquiry about your personal growth? I have explored my beliefs with the inquiry into the nature of self-love and radical self-love, the inquiry into healing, releasing, and the filling of that empty space where I feel void of the nurturing and caring I crave.

Life is such a constant opportunity to learn and grow. I had to know what I needed to work out for myself that could help me learn self-love.

Over a year ago, I was made an offer, an offer I had longed for; an offer I took no time to assess, evaluate, or do any discovery around. I knew when I first kissed this woman half my age, I was in deep trouble. I knew even then, this relationship would have a short shelf life, but the deep tingling throughout my body overrode all logical sense. I wanted what she was offering. I wanted every promise spoken and alluded to. I hung onto the fantasy of possibility.

My heart was cracked wide open, and I wanted it. I wanted to know love, lust, touch, erotica. I wanted to share a bed, swim with the skin of another like a dolphin, alongside another consenting adult. I had wished for it, dreamed for it, visualized what it would feel like to touch again. I had called her in.

Maybe I hadn't been specific enough with the details. Like someone closer to my age, with something we shared, the possibility of a match somewhere in the making. But no, I lacked a few details and in flirting with this energy exchange, I would be offered a basket of lessons. Lessons I pray I will remember next time around.

What follows is an expression of what I was feeling after the decision to separate and the flurry of insane thoughts that generated my internal emotional response.

Toxic lust. A bitter elixir.

I felt heartbreak that made no sense. It was illogical, and painful because of its allusions. It felt like a sickness, a virus contaminating my heart. The anger and the passion flared simultaneously. Two types of heat—one that nurtured me, the other that burned me up. I found myself juggling the two emotions like hot coals scarring my psyche. What was happening? I did not know what to do with this anger that starts as a spark and the flares up, burning at my toxic desire. It fueled me. It fed the passion yet to be expressed. It raised the lust once again.

And I wept over the loss of that nectar I am so addicted to. It was never sweet. It was always a bitter elixir.

Our time together was mostly filled with promise. There were small drops of kindness, measured responses, calculated restrictions and the constant lure of what could come. The lure intoxicated me. I followed it like a drug dependent addict.

Therein lies the shame for me. Within the desire, within the awareness of the toxic exchange, within the anger that could consume me, I could not feed you nor serve you.

The pain from your past wounds functioned as a ghost fueling our separation. Someone in your past had stolen parts of you, so I was not to be the recipient of your fullness. Thus, I became an intruder; a reminder of what was lost. A remembrance of how much you wanted love, but a reminder that your sexuality would be taken without permission, without consent. Your desire was fueled with the embers of a past not yet healed. My yearning was fueled by the allure of your body being given to me without prejudice within the explicit yes.

What will become of me and my burning passion? I carry a mark of loss on my heart. What will become of me? How can I recover from the pain of this toxic elixer making me insane with this lost relationship?

My Dragon Wakes

Where is the heat coming from?
The tingling, the fire, the arousal?
I hunger.
I hunger in such a deep way,
I cannot identify in total truth,
That for which I hunger.

Then in a flicker,
In the twinkle of an eye, the surge of a memory,
Abruptly, I am aware of that for which I hunger,
The cravings that never get quenched.
And then it rises like a dragon,
Flames bursting out,
In anger, joy, and confusion.
What has it taken from me to deny this truth?

I am one who marches on.
In the moment,
I know not how to feed this hunger,
This desire, this deepest of needs.
I march on.
Then one day,
In a flicker, a wink, a smile,
My dragon speaks,
"Say yes, you fool, say yes."

Our Yes was Sacred

Our yes was sacred.

Yes, is the expression of an unfolding.
Yes, is beyond grasping.
This yes is a no holding back from desire: YES.
I said yes to you,

The exploration of you.

I had a hunger, a deep empty well.
With you, I said yes, to my list, my desire.
The presence of my yes, answered with your yes.

I needed the flow and fluidity within the yes.
I wanted to experience your yes,
To fill my hunger with your exquisite yes.
We both poured out our desire,
Into the yes and the yes only, into the explicit yes.
We played in the unknown, we explored,
We went on the adventure of yes.

The hunger fed,

We dove in deeper.

The well received, the sacred.

I got to have you,

The rise of our desire, the juice, the lust.
The sensuality of our sex in the explicit yes.
That sacred yes that healed.
Grateful for the reminder.
Yes, you are desired.
Yes, you have vitality.

Yes, you are alive in your needs.

As the hunger got filled,
The yes began to fade,
The desire lost once fed.

And then the yes was gone.
The adventure gone.
The well filled.
The sacred work complete.
In the sacred yes,

We move on.

Skin on Skin

Skin on skin.

The yearning.
The sensations, the feeding.
I seek the intimacy, the truth of contact.
I seek the presence, the being of the moment.
I seek to let go of the armor, the story.
The micro expressions that say, "No."
All the ways I say "No" to being loved.
I seek the fullness of being alive.

Skin on Skin.
The yearning.
Energized.

Creativity surging, pulsating,
As the kundalini rises.

Eye to eye.
The truth of souls journeying through time and space.

The exponential expansion that feeds my humanity.
I seek a truth with you that I have not fully embraced for myself,
Not because you are that truth, but the mirror that lets me see.
See beyond that which I have yet to own.
I seek your lips on mine; juicy,
Driving into all the lust of my heart, bodies merging.

I seek YES
And skin on skin is such a small part of the seeking.
I seek to allow.

To say "Yes," and to be in integrity with the yes.
To be nurtured, and healed by the yes, by the touch.

Let Me

Let me investigate your soul
Let me peak at the heart of my lover
And see how to love you more.

Let me hold the moment
Nurture that which we will not forget
So, we will not hate each other when we end.

Let me say you are amazing
And show you I mean it
Let me show you what self-love looks like
When I agree to self-care
And not let up on how I show up for self-care.

Let me take you in,
Take you in so deeply,
So completely that
What needs to be healed is healed.

Let me touch your soft, wet lips
And in that moment
Let me surrender to
How much I crave your
Tenderness, your nectar.

Let me hold you in my heart,
With no attachment.

For in this state
Our shared love has space to grow,
To go from a seed of desire,
To a full pledged, embodied answered dream.

Let me remind you; love is a job,
It is the inner work of self-love first,
Self-care and self-acceptance.

Let me remind you; this thing we have is
A point in the universe when
Two forces collide to change
The very nature of what the universe holds.

Let me say this;
You, my love, inspire me to be more me.
You, my love, show me how heart trumps everything.
You, my love, light up my heart
And that heart then shines brighter in the world.
To love myself more deeply,
And in the doing of that, love others more completely.

I love Our Bodies in the Explicit Yes

So empty, so void of touch,
That intimate touch,
A lover's touch, the breath that fills your soul,
Inhaling the sensual nature, the skin, the sweat, the juice,
Filling the barren space within.

That space had dried up like the floor of a sunbaked desert,
Harsh in its emptiness.
The soul aches from the hunger.
Passion matters, touch, deep,
Emerging in the juices of lust, fire ignited.
Oh, how I love my mouth on lips,
Hips touching, my nipples hardening,
The sensation of you surging through my skin.

I love our bodies in the explicit Yes,
The throwing open, heated in the exchange.
I love your body in the explicit Yes,
Searching to be me with my passion,
Explicit into the moist cave,
The flooding smells that ache for response.

How my love may I serve you?
For it is in the serving of you,
I feed a part of me yet to be fed,
Yet to be filled by explicitness.
How may I serve you dear one?
My tongue seeks to land,
My hands tingling with desire,
Eyes feasting with anticipation.

I seek to serve us both in the explicit Yes.

In the In Between Spaces

In the in-between spaces

There is a fragrance
That cannot be held or grasped.
It slips between the fingers,
Floats out of reach.

In the in-between spaces

I feel the softness,
The fragrance
Touching my heart.
Drop into the fragrance
That is tangible within the ether.
The touch, the intent, the heart, the scent.

In the in-between spaces

The fragrance travels
Through time, space
And reincarnations
To unite us,
To reawaken the lineage of partnership,
The bonds that the ether holds.

In the in-between spaces

You have found me.
I recognize the fragrance,
I am flooded with memories.
The yearning,
The longings to consume,
To replenish
Your presence in my heart,

To presence your heart with mine.

In the in-between spaces

The fragrance unites us,
Love lost is found,
Remembered as possible once again.

I suggest that last paragraph:
I feel loved,
Once again.
The love is made tangible
In the in-between spaces.

The Cliff

Scorched by Trauma

It's a cone of silence, a wall, a division. How can two people live so close and not have anything to do with each other? There is a physical wall between bedrooms, an emotional wall between bedrooms, an emotional wall between ex-lovers. A psychic wall between the wounded. It's painful, absurd, and yet necessary. How do we get past what has been projected onto this situation, onto each other? This is a story borne from pain, abuse, and fears. A story so deep in each other's history I did not see it coming.

There were direct references and stories we told each other about the common mistreatments we experienced called "life as a female" and "childhood objectification at every turn." We created the illusion that boundaries between us were being respected.

I don't know what happened. These reactive responses, yours, and mine, the PTSD I have been asking to heal are being pushed in my face. It breaks my heart to see you stuck in the behavioral pattern, a powerless three-year-old, lashing out at me as if I were your abuser, enemy, attacker, and violator. The shame settles into me like ink seeping into the paper this story is told on.

Oh, how my heart hurts that I am being projected upon so fiercely.

All my inner child wants is to be loved, to be seen, to be held. But instead, here I stand with my wounds fiercely ripped open, and I ache from the fear and the shame of not knowing how to be different or how to protect the child within me. This woman is a walking trauma, scorching my soul with the venom of the toxic violations inflicted on her body, mind, and soul.

I stand in my kitchen frozen in time, speechless, afraid to move lest it yet again provoke another verbal attack, another accusation of, "You're doing it wrong!" I have lost my confidence and am revisited by sharp memories of losing my sense of self once again. I stand frozen without a single clue what to do.

I called up to Spirit, "What have I done? How could I be this bad person, this person accused of harming another when all I wanted was to be loved, to love, be held and to hold? How, dear God, did I fall into the accusation of the abuser? How can I protect my place, my inner child, and my self-worth under this forceful attack driven by fear and pain?"

So, I step away, I stop talking, I stand tall even when I want to run and hide. And at times, I do hide by staying in my bedroom and waiting 'till the coast is clear to cook my food and take care of other household chores. Yet the force of projection continues, and I endure constant anger and madness, and the rejection of even the slightest human kindness.

Time. Yes, time will be my friend. It gives me a chance to self-evaluate, to re-evaluate, to revisit what is being offered. What can I learn? What can I heal? What can I own and what can I change?

My mind swirling, my heart aching and my emotions erupting. I feel so angry! It is my way to fight back, to call out the intensity of feelings, to reject this projection to give back the self-loathing I have taken on. I feel so ashamed having failed this woman I wanted to love, wanted to nurture, and support in her healing. But I did not understand the healing I need to go through myself and the scarring I must recover from if I am to reclaim my sense of self and claim a place of self-love.

I knew when I entered this addiction, I would have lessons presented. With all lessons, they take the perfect form, at the perfect time as an answer to the spoken and unspoken quest for growth.

As I continue to share a wall and put up my walls, I can only ask that I not let this woman's pain exclude me from my joy of living. I must not allow her paranoia to infect my life any further. What boundary do I set? She has declared hers with sharp edges, a rigid bubble she has put around herself. I pray not to get cut by her penetrating hatred of me, to not lose my soul to her loathing.

In the end, what will I do? What learning will unfold?

For now, I keep the vigils of self-care and self-love. And then there's my ever present "Fuck you, you bitch! I will not be mastered by your pain and your self-loathing!"

Oops! Still fucking angry and for now that's a good thing!

Oh, So Needy

You told me, I was needy
You told me, do not expect you to nurture me.
You told me, my needs would not be met by you.
You told me, "Learn to feed your needs yourself."

I was confused.

Are we in a relationship, lovers, sisters, friends?
What are we?
I was trained, told, enforced to serve others first.
My needs were at the bottom of a long list.

From early on, I was my mother's helper,
My mother's legs, my mother's mother.

And you want what from me?
You want me to consciously choose not to do what?

What?

I got curious.
I turned around and reviewed my life.
I bought love, been trained to buy love,
Use acts of service to buy love,
And you want me not to what?

Oh change!

Yet deep in my cells I am programed, I am not worthy.
I must provide for others. How else will I earn love?
Change the way I love and receive love,
The love you so strongly reject.

I turned in the direction of that programming.

Sought out help.
I had a profound experience,
I saw what you were seeing.
In plain sight to you, totally blindsiding me.

Reminiscent of the child's story book,
"Are You My Mother?"
Buried deep was the longing of an infant to be nurtured.

Well, there you have it, I was needy.

So unconsciously needy, I subconsciously called in a healer.
She came disguised as a lover, witch and far too often a bitch.
I took on just as much discomfort as my body, mind, psyche could manage,
I dove in to rescue myself.
Learning self-love took another upward turn.

Yes, I am looking for love.

And as the growth and process continues
I am sure someone will find me needy another time.

Who knows what growth that will bring?
I am certain, it will be made known to me.

I Smell You

I smell you in my cells.
I so want to release you.
Release you from being the source of my desire,
The ache that penetrates my heart,
The fulfillment of my hunger.
I stand in the bravado of "I'm OK."
But you know what?
I am Not.

Nasty, Nasty, Nasty

You have been a nasty girl.

Your tongue is like a blade cutting through my sanity.
Nasty, fierce protector of your gaping wound.
Your fierceness slices through any reasoning,
Any inquiry, any place we could stand on different ground.

Nasty is your protector.

Once your scar has been jarred, the pus that lay beneath began to ooze out.
The nasty smell of your fear, the penetrating color of your mistrust,
And the constant attachment to control.
Nasty to live with, unnerving because of your energetic loudness.
I felt you coming in, the unpredictable, your pain ruling every interaction,
With no concessions, absolutely no concessions.

What happened to the kindness that lovers have?
What happened to the soft place that helped us face the world?

As the pus seeps out, there is a hope of the wounds healing,
But alas only a hope.

The deeply entrenched response comes from a child,
A child scared and helpless.
What is the bridge that needs to be built here?
The bridge that crosses over to your adult,
The bridge that empowers you, the kind one,
You, the reasonable one?

This journey towards healing has you fighting everything, on all fronts.
I am not your enemy, though I see you scanning for proof that I am unsafe.
I turned into your unsafe place.
What am I to do with this nasty, trauma that pierces us both?

Narcissistic shit! What is the lesson here?
What is the healing here?
How do I release you from my energetic body?
My physical body, my psychic body?

I have memories I replay.
My heart wants something I had with you.
It was short, but it opened me up to something,
Something that needs feeding that I don't know how to feed.

I am in the desert wanting to quench the thirst.
How do I release myself from you?

How Sick Am I?

The problem is you are addictive.
In all your toxic wounds, I miss you.
You're hard to navigate, your boundaries difficult to keep up.
I have been shamed by you, belittled by you,
Made wrong by you and treated like a child by you.

And yet I long for that part of us that only stayed a short time.
As we poured the hose of hunger down our throats,
We were infatuated with the explorations.
I am left with the infatuation and not much else.
You in your pain, you cut me out,
Controlled the narrative.

Silenced my voice, controlled all the things,
All the things that you could not control as an abused child.
You cut me out for fear of feeling me love you with attachment,
Loving you in service to your sexual hunger,
My sexual hunger.

And then I was severed as if I was the problem,
Because in your world I had become the problem.
I yell, I refuse your option, I refuse your total unbending control.
I refuse to comply to your dictator's rule.
And so fuck it, I want to service you anyway.
How sick am I? Fuck!

There's a Ghost Walking Around in the Attic of my Memories.

There's a ghost walking around in the attic of my memories,
Stirring up the dust, the particles of pain that settled in my heart.
Stirring up a cloud of emotions I had stored.
I want to stop feeling, feeling the loss of you.
Then you walk around in the attic reminding me of the mistakes I made with you,
Reminding me of the desire I miss because you're gone.
I want the dust to settle,
The memories to get covered by the pain that hides the grief and shame.
You are leaving footprints in the dust of these memories,
A ghost that refuses to leave, refuses to be kind,
A ghost determined to torture my heart with regrets.
Faced with impossible choices, a death happened, and the grieving continues.

There's a ghost walking around in the attic of my memories,
If only, if only a wish.
I wish I had spoken more clearly, told more truths, asked more questions,
Set more boundaries.
If only my apologies were accepted, my love seen as a gift not a threat,
If only.
But alas, the ghost is staying, walking on the floorboards of the promises made, the hopes lost the dreams unfulfilled.

The ghost refusing to relinquish its punishment of me,
For not doing better, for failing to know the signs,
For failing to create a safe place in your own body for you to reside.
This ghost lives in my pain, is fed by my grief.
I want to yell-GO AWAY!

And yet I know it will not, for the lessons offered have yet to be claimed.
This ghost knows I am still not able to fill my heart with self–love,
Not enough to force it out.
Soon, I say, soon.

Until then,
The ghost remains in the attic of my memories.
And one day it will evaporate into the sunlight.
Giving me the chance to forgive, forget and move on.

The Work

The Dreamer

As a child I had dreams of things I would do, things I would become. They didn't seem like dreams beyond my reach. They were big dreams, small dreams, dreams for the future. They were not impossible or beyond reach dreams. I was told they were not to be dreamed and that I was not the one who would access these dreams. But in private I dreamed these dreams anyway.

As a child, the wonder and innocence of dreaming fueled a void I felt from living in a small town. A town with small minds and little vision for any future I could seek for myself. And yet, I desperately wanted these dreams! I wanted to know the texture of wealth and of abundance. I knew it must have a look, a touch, and a smell I longed to know. I wanted to be on an adventure, exploring different dimensions of what life had to offer. I wanted to experience the colors, shapes, and sounds of other cultures.

I was told so often that I was a dreamer. It was spoken with hardness, said as a punishment. These criticisms were meant to keep me in my place. After all, who was I to want, to speak of a place rich with different possibilities? Who was I indeed?

My mother was afraid for me. Somehow, in her mind, to dream was dangerous, unsafe, unforgiving. The way she saw it, her job was to make sure I did not get too big for my britches. I was not to embarrass her with my antics of a world that –OMG dare I say it? –included me! That was too big of a dream. That I would see someone in the outer world who I could recognize, who was like me.

My mom was put on a boat when she was twelve years old. She was sent off to work for a family she did not know, separated from her twelve brothers and sisters, put to work as an indentured servant. Did my mother dream? Did her dreams end in disappointment? I never heard my mother speak about anything beyond the daily survival grind she lived in. And trust me she was in the grind as a house cleaner, a nanny, a mother, and a wife.

I could sense how trapped she felt in her life, the real lack of options. The one dream she seemed to allow herself was for her children, for them to have a better life through education and options. But aside from that, my dreams scared her somehow. She could not understand them and why I wanted a world so different from hers, a life beyond where she would be included.

I spent a lot of time dreaming up where I would change and grow my life. You see, dreaming is a very big step toward living in your passion. How could I be creative, see possibilities if I could not dream?

Then there was the very real way that my dreams worked in my life to take me into a subconscious journey, into alpha beta mind set where I was given amazing visions of what I was to do. It was so palpable that I would wake with absolute clarity of its message. And should I slack in its directive, I would surely get a knock from the universe to push me into action inspired by that dream.

Right now, at this time in my life, I am laughing so hard at what others told me to do or not to do when it comes to my dreaming and using my imagination. As our collective consciousness rises, we as a society, are being taught the importance of having a dream. Mentors, coaches, and guides are taking people into the world of creating their dreams and working with the divine mind within each of us to crate the life their desire draws them toward.

All things created in this world are done first from thought, then from form. Think about it. When haven't you ever really done anything that ou first had the idea, then you acted on it? That is what makes choosing your dreams so powerful.

The creative use and belief in our power to visualize our lives is creating momentous changes in this world right now. It will take more of us believing in our abilities as source to dream up this new order of equality, inclusivity, and respect for all things. What about that perfect job, or new car, or the ideal lover, all of it comes from the power of how you use your mind.

I am a dreamer. I love what I am dreaming up next. How about you? How are you using your dreams to create your best life?

A Child's Wish

I have a memory,
A scent, a tingling, a sensation,
Riding on the wave of a wish.
This scent reveals a longing,
Something has gone missing.
Then a wave smashes against the memory,
Waking up the lost.
A loss which was never claimed,
A part of self, left abandoned, left in fear.
A child's wish for love.
The fear of never knowing it.
Never knowing exceptional love.
Never knowing unconditional love.
Never knowing a mother's love.

My light will shine

I am veiled.
My light is muted and dimmed.
Yet, I am shining brightly,
Behind this mask of fear.
Fear has woven around me a film to hide my true nature.
I hide for fear of my brilliance,
I hide for fear of recognition,
The recognition that would ask my light to shine brighter still.
I dread this veil staying too long,
For behind it I ache to be seen in my fullness.
Can that be handled – my illumination?

I am veiled.
The particles of dust that shield me
Now are remnants of past wounds,
Stories that feed the illusions of separation.
This veil persists,
Yet, I shine behind it with the prayer that one day
I will burn away the separation,
Be seen in my full illumination.
I am that bright light.
As the veil releases,

Change is the blessing.

Will I Do What I Am Meant to Do?

My wings are tucked tightly,
Holding on.
My dream is unfolding,
I am waiting to go.
Do I run to the cliff and jump?
Do I hope my wings will unfold?

Will I fly?

Will they carry me?

Do I dare test them,
In front of God and everyone,
Uncertain of their willingness?
Will they do what they are meant to do?
Will I do what I am meant to do?

Let's test it and jump!

In the Sweet Moments

In the sweet moments,
In the silence of the deep dark night,
I remember who I am.
I am, in the I am
The deep silence, of the deep darkness
A journey into a part of self that cannot be visible in the daylight

It is a soft shell,
It is sensitive skin,
It is pain held in the reflection of others,
In the deep darkness
In the silence of the night,
I hear an echo of what I am
What I could be.

In its vibration and reverberation,
It sends out its message.
I am, that's all.
I am in the deep depths of me.
I am the source of all that I do, that I feel, that I see.

I am in the darkness that holds me
As a cloak wrapped around me
Silence in the darkness nurtures me
For in that moment, in that quiet,
In that peace, I am nurtured.

There is a longing that emerges in that quiet,
Longing to show up in that peace,
In that quiet, in the daylight,
In the exchanges, in the conversations.

I long to be open,
To receive, nurture, believe

This longing that holds me close,
Reminds me of my aliveness.
In this longing I am choosing the I am as life itself.

The Whispers Fly by in the Ether

The whispers fly by in the ether.
What? What was that?
Is that the answer or another question?

You start to chase after it,
That illusive whisper, hoping it offers a solution
Or at least a given quantity to a given thing.

But No! In that fleeting moment,
You have already lost the intent behind the whisper.
You go back to the mundane, fixing lunch and watching Netflix.
And then somewhere between the loading of the dishwasher,
And chewing on the carrot there comes another whisper.

This time it stays longer.
This time you get to grab it by the tail as it flies by.
This time you hold on and you pray, pray with all your heart.
This time you will feel the answer in your body,
Feel it so deeply it grounds itself in your consciousness.

The whisper materializes, the spark of inspiration takes hold.
With a deep breath, this whisper transforms you.
This whisper turns from a longing to understanding, into the act of now you know.
It is in this moment where the dedication to consciousness,
The raising yourself to be more, become more.

And just then a whisper flies by the ether, and it starts all over again
This is the nature of consciousness.
Fleeting moments sometimes captured;
But more often than not,
You're just chasing with the hope that once again
you'll grab its tail and fly.

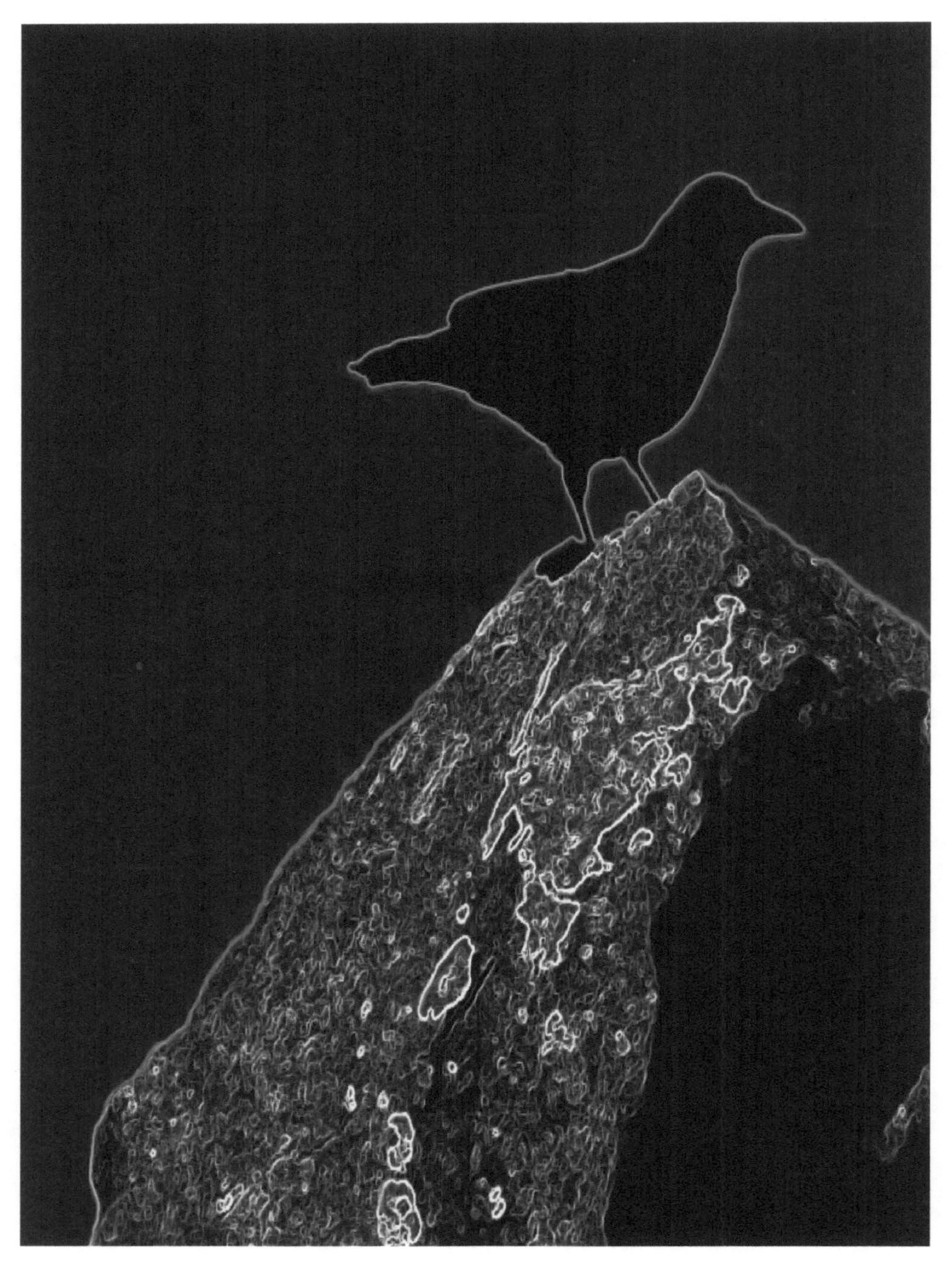

Raven

Raven smashed into the window of my dream
Penetrating the ethers of my mind.
Why had you come bruised, black, blue, broken?
Your wing snapped from abuse,
You began to tell your story,
One line, one glance, one withdrawal at a time.
It was hard not to weep openly, intensely, unapologetically,
As you entered my private domain with your pain.

To most your story would be cloaked,
This glittering iridescence of your majestic stature.
You Raven, full of magic,
Forced into breaking, forced to summit.
Repeatedly violated, repeatedly cornered,
Repeatedly released from personal agreement.

You smashed into the inner sanctum of my dream,
Your magic will not cloak you here.
By smashing through my shield, you entered
My domain, my magic.

There you are in the quiet space
Within the shield of my dream,
The sacred boundary of self, articulated.

There is a YOU that will emerge from the solace of this time to heal.
The mending will be invisible,
I will not be its viewer.
For you, Raven, cloaked in your glittering iridescence
Hold the shape of you.

You smashed into the window of my dream,
To become your own dream.
To claim that dream which is you.

The Healing

Pushing the Mountain

I have tried to push the mountain, using my will to challenge the obstacles in front of me. Pushing as hard as I could so as not to fail. I pushed myself, pushed to prove my worth, pushed to achieve greater success than my parents. Pushed to match my brother's gift for academics. I pushed to not be defined by others. I pushed to breathe a part of myself I can identify with. There has been too much brainwashing. I was unconscious of how much I was acting from this deep brainwashing. It's exhausting, I'm exhausted.

All that pushing, a pattern learned as a value, a way to prove my value. All the while it's so not what Spirit wants for me. On this journey of becoming, I get to practice another way. All the programing, beliefs, and patterns I get to release and create new ones.

Here's how I start. I stop pushing the mountain! I cannot push the mountain, but I can float down the river that's born of the mountain. I can enjoy the ease of the water carrying me to what is and always has been the ease in which I can be in live.

Breathe, just breathe. Life is for me, not against me.

Today I remind myself I am the source of all the good. I am manifesting and receiving. Today I get to look behind me and ask, "What new muscle have I claimed on this journey, this time?"

As I travel on this road called life, I have been a seeker, a quester on the search for truth, purpose of life. I have wondered so often what is this thing known as ease and flow. It is not something I have been able to embrace for it's not something I feel without a lot of conscious practice on my part. I have been in the practice of pushing the mountain.

With great desire and joy in my heart I have started a new practice. It is about leading with my heart. What does my heart want? And my heart wants ease. My heart wants to trust in the great flow of all things. What I want wants me. And so, it is, new opportunity to grow presented itself. And with this vision, new practice, I get to allow what life wants from me to happen. I am blessed and I am grateful. And the mountain is very content standing right where it is.

Who knew?

Back to Me

The shift is happening.
I recognized it today,
I could not feel you penetrate my being.
I felt it today,
The emptying out of you from my body.
It was subtle and soft,
Vapors floating out of my cells.

A peace came over me,
A calm I had not felt in a long time.
I have not forgotten you,
I will not lose sight of the lesson you brought.
There is a gratefulness,
This shift has happened.
There is a freedom of breath.

Back to me,
I recognize the being I have become.

A Seed Believes

Can you smell the richness of the soil?
The aliveness of spring,
Buds pushing against the moisture of possible.
New beginnings held up by ritual,
Seeds planted long before the breaking of ground
Or the vision of what is to come.

Can you smell the clarity of purpose?
The expression of destiny that a seed believes,
Not with a conscious intention,
But with an instinct so richly embedded it has no choice.
What seed is planted in you?
You can feel its cravings,
The need for fulfillment.
Can you smell its destiny in you?
You are the richness,
The soil that births the seed,
A seed believes.

What travels through time and space?

There was a time when my moccasins touched Mother Earth and I felt her beneath me. I knew the scent of spring as she greeted me with the awakening of something new. I felt my roots growing into the earth beneath me and connecting me to the soul of my own potential.

Mother Earth guided me through the seasons of my life with the love a mother has for her child. And when I forgot to treat her with respect; she forgave me. "You are learning child, and you have so much to discover."

My moccasins traveled over long distances through time and space, reminding me I am a child of this earth. And when I listen, truly listen, I know how to greet each day with the reverence and respect it deserves. When I open my eyes to truly see, I perceive the connections among all living things, and I know my part in all of this.

As I stand with my feet planted on this earth, I am part of the creation of all that is sacred. My moccasins planted on this earth will keep me grounded in this awakening and awareness.

The Dancer Dances

The Dancer dances, spinning, spiraling
The texture of her spirit moving the fabric of her life.
Her royal presence intrigues you and calls you forward.
This Dancer ascends,
Her crown bowing to cosmic grace,
Flowing, strength and prosperity.

The Dancer dances, movement flowing
From every cell of her passion.
Moving with joy, sadness, pain, and remorse the Dancer dances.
It is her survival; it is how she thrives.
The fabric of her being demands the dance.
Shines in the light of the beloved glance.

The Dancer dances,
Her partner's bow into her heart,
And the magnificence radiates out
Bursting opens the soul's delight, for all to partake.

The Dancer dances, it must be shared,
For it is divine guidance speaking through her muscles,
Her outstretched limbs, her torso, lean and muscular.
The beauty of her dance drawing you in.
She speaks of the magic of life through her body,
Her heart, her movement, the divine grace that lives within.
The Dancer dances so we may know joy, healing and
The greatest connection of all the Divine moving through us.

I am In the I am

My brother named me Brenda,
My mother named me Rebecca,
My father named me Bryan, in the patriarchal tradition.

But who I am is in, the I am.
I am…
A seeker, an innovator, an eco-feminist, an activist, a peacenik
An advocate of human rights,
A fool,
A sensitive poet,
An elder, sage, hag, ball buster.

I am in the I am.
I am…
A guide,
A humorist,
Spiritualist,
A speaker, a communicator, a coach,
A teacher, a student.

I am in the I am.
I am
A dancer
A lover,
A problem solver,
A magical child,
A meditator,
A storyteller,
I am the story.
A wearer of many hats,
A lover of life.
Who I am is in the I am.
I am a big-hearted woman out to change the world,
One good deed at a time.

There is a Breath

There is a breath, breathing me.
It blows through me,
Like the wind coaxing the leaves to speak in tongues,
A language spoken by the laws of the universe.
It is a force so powerful,
Its true power is yet to be revealed.
When it breathes through me
It comes as a whisper,
Disguising its deepest potential.

There's a breath breathing me.
It whispers my potential to me.
Divine ideas knocking on my awareness.
It tingles, as memory, as a noticing.
It can start quiet,
Low key, stealth in its nature.
How stealth it really is depends on my noticing.
Its voice is as loud as my desire to hear.

This breath of the divine breathing through me,
A new awakening, a vision searching to be expressed.
I rise within this breath of life.
I dance within the breath,
To move, to deepen the breath within.
My divine nature starts to expand.
New desire dances in the spaciousness of the breath.
The breath that breathes me, brings me life.
Life filled with desire, creativity, passion.
This breath flows through me, it is the wind in a reed,
Making sweet, sweet music of my life.

Golden Flaws – Embracing Flaws and Imperfections

Kintsugi the Japanese art of putting broken pottery pieces back together with gold, built on the idea that in embracing flaws and imperfections you can create an even stronger, more beautiful piece of art.

My heart was broken. It felt like I was shattered into pieces. Yet, I was surprised how liberating it was. The releasing of all that pain held there for years. I was blindsided by its impact.

I chose to say yes to a delicious offer of sexual intimacy and love. I went full steam ahead into what I knew to be a dangerous choice. And yet all I knew was I wanted what was offered. I wanted this lustful, irrational experience. I said yes to what felt like a new possibility, a new perspective, an adventure in pushing my limitations. I wanted 'it,' this inviting package of intrigue and opportunity.

Upon reflection, it was a familiar pattern running itself yet again. It became a journey of discovery. I was privileged to see a side of myself I had hidden from the world. I also saw a side of myself that I had no real awareness of how I was expressing it. I found it difficult to cut through my line of defenses. I was flooded with stimulations, they confused me, aroused me, heightened by sense and imagination. Chaos ruled as I scrambled to get my footing in this new terrain, I scrambled to hear her needs, to connect in ways that were meaningful to her and to have my own wants and needs met. At its best, we were discovering each other. During its worst, what felt right and safe had flown out the window.

I was seeking love from all the wrong places. I had developed a pattern from my early relationship with my mother. She was not someone who would nurture me. She loved me but as I became more able, she relied on me to take care of her, nurture her. I was more her mother than she was mine. I would enter this new relationship completely unaware of the wounded child who was seeking someone to love her.

My lover knew and she was repelled by it. I was left feeling totally frustrated in our exchanges. I really did not understand what she was repelled by. I lived with this as part of my composition for an exceedingly long time. And now with this woman, I was shamed by her for this side of me. My inner child was showing herself in a way that violated the code of adult sexuality, or responsible adulting.

I had not been aware of this. These behaviors had never stood out this painfully before. As hindsight is, I could look at my other partnerships and see the unfolding. I was totally astounded by this new crack in my self-awareness.

They say that when something breaks inside, something else can seep out. That's what it felt like as I engaged with the inner workings that demand my attention. I had my heart broken. A relationship turned upside down. I asked for this growth, but so unable to tame it as it took hold of my sensibilities. That chaos meant I could no longer keep the façade that had been hiding *me*. I was falling apart. It was a prayer being answered. I was now able to see myself as the imperfect reflection of my human journey. My flaws and imperfections were my beauty. This shifted my consciousness.

I have always felt flawed. I have always pushed to exert my place, to believe in my own voice, and my own worth. It all came spilling out when this heart broke for all the right reasons. This long held painful inner view was flawed. It needed to be released. I needed this releasing and healing.

The Kintsugi technique is an extension of the Japanese philosophy of

wabi-sabi, which sees beauty in the incomplete and value in simplicity.

The aesthetic is sometimes described as one of beauty that is

"Imperfect, impermanent, and incomplete."

I set about the work of putting the broken pieces back together again. Something important had happened. I got to know deeply a side of myself that had been calling to me for a long time. A part of me that whispered and screamed at the same time. I stepped into a truth I had not seen in myself. A child left abandoned to fend for herself, and an adult lost to her own inability to self-nurture. I finally understood the significant impact it had created in intimate relationships. The amazing sense of finally getting it, its behaviors, subtle stories, and invested perspective of who I thought I was.

I was not seeing a truth about myself. It was time to pick up the pieces and fill the cracked, flawed parts of me with gold. That gold was the self-love I had never known that I could apply to myself. That gold was the awareness that I was a child of the infinite, always spiraling to a greater Becoming.

These poems and essays are what seeped out of me. This was a creative process that healed my heart and so many other wounds in my life. It opened a space I had not seen before.

This heartbreak was the journey home to self that was so unexpected. She opened my eyes and heart to a new perspective I had been praying for. I learned that when I embraced my flaws, they were my gold. And that who I am and the life I have lived are the things that make me unique and precious.

This opportunity that broke my heart also freed parts of me that needed to spill out, needed to be set free, and needed to be seen. And released that uniquely beautiful aspect of me needing to be loved. In the midst of challenging relationship issues, what had felt so painful, taught me to embrace my flaws and imperfections.

This journey was the gold to becoming stronger and embracing the beautiful lessons—and soul healing.

"Raise your Voice to Change the World."

Your voice matters and I support you raising that voice to become the impactful influence you are meant to be. I empower women to transform their lives by shifting their beliefs, behaviors and patterns keeping them from living in their passion by working from the inside out.

I graduated as a Communications Designer from the Nova Scotia College of Art and Design. This education set me up to be creative and innovative in all areas of life. I refer to myself as a renaissance woman. After a short and frightening experience working under an oppressive system in the corporate world, I took my skills to the nonprofit world. I joined the second wave of the Women's Movement. After years of political activity, the disparity my community felt when our actions failed to create any change had me looking for a different means to create change. I read the book, "Working from the Inside Out" by Sonia Johnson, which changed my approach to everything I did. From that point on, I recognized the need for tools that would change the world through the inner work that reflected the outer consciousness.

What's Brenda up to now?

Brenda is a kick ass speaker with a passion for the empowerment of women. She is a dynamic, passionate, and knowledgeable keynote and workshop leader. Her warm-hearted, humorous style has an innate way of having each person feel like she knows them. As a natural born storyteller, she paints pictures with words that draw you into the moment and create an environment where the audience feels connected and seen. She can engage a room. Her life experience gives her a deep wisdom as a facilitator, teacher and leader who can read and lead a room.

Check out her website at BrendaRBryan.com

CPSIA information can be obtained
at www.ICGtesting.com
Printed in the USA
BVHW021955220822
645226BV00007B/64

* 9 7 8 0 5 7 8 3 7 3 7 2 0 *